Playtime Learning Games for Young Children

Playtime Learning Games
for Young Children

ALICE S. HONIG

SYRACUSE UNIVERSITY PRESS

00   10 9 8 7 6

Library of Congress Cataloging in Publication Data

Honig, Alice S.
  Playtime learning games for young children.

  1. Educational games. I. Title.
GV1480.H66 1982   649′.68   82-16794
ISBN 0-8156-0178-6 (pbk.)

Manufactured in the United States of America

CONTENTS

EVERYDAY WAYS TO ENRICH
    YOUR CHILD'S LEARNING   7

Learning Tasks for Young Children   7

Tips for Getting the
    Most out of Learning Games   20

PLAYTIME LEARNING GAMES
    FOR YOUNG CHILDREN   25

THE GAMES   27

1   People We Know   27

2   Laundry Lists   30

3   How Many Things Can You Tell Me
    about This?   34

4   Water Games   36

5   Guessing Differences: A Sentence
    Completion Game   41

6   Egg Carton Color Cups   44

7   Stories and Songs   48

8   Food Names   53

9   First Place–Last Place   56

10   Sounds Game   58

11   How Else Could You Use This Toy?
    An Imagination Game   61

12   Where Will My Doggie Sit? A Space
       Words Game   64
13   The Feely Box   67
14   A What, Where, When, How, Why Game   71
15   Cooking Eggs: How Materials Change   77
16   Gingerbread Man   82
17   Catching a Silly Question: A Learning
       to Listen Game   86
18   Frog Friends: A Counting Game   89
19   Which Things Do We Do First?   92
20   Helper around the House   95
21   Are There More or Fewer?
       A Comparing Game   99
22   Same and Different: How to Make and
       Line Up Groups   103
23   Neighborhood Explorations   110
24   Social Skills   113

EVERYDAY WAYS TO ENRICH YOUR CHILD'S LEARNING

Every parent wants his or her child to be a good learner. Yet sometimes you might wonder how you can help your young child learn. Isn't that supposed to be a teacher's job? Indeed it is. And you, the parent, are your child's first teacher. You are your child's most loved and most important teacher.

This book contains games that are learning activities for children from age two through kindergarten age. These games will be easy for your child and you to play. You do not need fancy toys. You can do many of these games *while** you are getting daily chores done. Your child's learning takes place while you are busy together taking care of household jobs. When you are doing work in your home you will also be doing your "homework" as a parent — helping your child become a good learner!

Learning Tasks for Young Children

There are 12 learning tasks that are important for the

*A word is put in *italics* in this book because —
1. that word is especially important, or
2. you should emphasize that word as you speak to your child.

preschool age child. The games in this book will help you make sure that your child gets help with each of these learning tasks. Here are the learning tasks your preschooler will need to work on:

1. Learning to make groups

A young child finds it hard to understand why things go together. Games in this book show you how to help your child discover how things go together and why things go together. Your child will learn that some things go together because they —

- *sound* the same
- *taste* the same
- *feel* the same
- have the same *color*
- have the same *shape*
- are the same *length*
- are *made* of the same *stuff*
- are the same *size*
- are used together (cup and saucer or table and chair)
- are used for the same reason (couch, chair, and bench).

Children need to sharpen their noticing skills in order to make groups. Parents can help them *compare* the way things look or feel or taste or sound. You point out how things are the same or different. Children will then notice more details. You will be helping them get ready for school work. They will be better able to notice letters and numbers that look or sound the same or different.

2. Learning to see separate parts in a big group

Children have to learn about big groups. They need to know the names for big groups such as—

- furniture
- animals
- clothing
- family
- foods

But every big group has different parts. A family group has parents, children, grandparents, and other special people. There are many different kinds of flowers. There are many different kinds of dogs in the dog group. Yet dogs are only *one* kind of animal in the animal group. There are smaller groups inside bigger groups. For instance, cats and dogs and turtles are three groups inside one bigger group called "pet animals."

In learning to read, your child will have to learn that letters are parts of words. Words are grouped into sentences. Sentences make up stories.

3. Learning to line up objects in a logical order

Little children have to struggle to line up cars from the littlest to the biggest. They need your help in learning how to line up objects from—

- smoothest to bumpiest
- softest to loudest
- fattest to skinniest
- hardest to softest
- tallest to shortest
- wettest to driest

4. Learning how time goes

Young children get very confused about when things are supposed to happen. Games in this book will help you teach time words. Your child will learn the meaning of words like *before* and *after.* Your child may be more obedient if he or she has a clearer idea of what *soon* means.

5. Learning about places and how space is organized

Some grownups think that children naturally understand the meaning of *top* or *bottom, outside* or *around.* But your children need you to *act* out these space ideas with them. In games, your children will get *behind* the chair and *under* the table. They will find out what space and place ideas mean.

6. Learning what numbers mean

Preschool children can sometimes learn to count by rote in a sing song. But they need help in learning how to count objects or people or fingers or toes. Help your child begin to understand that each object in a pile or row can only be counted one time if you want to find out how many there are. As your child touches the last toe and says "ten," explain that the last number counted tells how many there are. So there are ten toes. Encourage your child to *touch* each item while counting. Count pennies, buttons or green peas. Count steps in walking. Count out enough cups for each person if your child is having juice with friends. Count the number of cookies you and your child place on a baking sheet before you put them in the oven.

Help your child use a calendar to count off the days in a month before his or her birthday or other special day.

Use words like *first*, *second*, and *third*. As you dry dishes or put away groceries, count with your child. "You are drying the first spoon. Now you are drying the second spoon." "The large plates go on the first shelf. The little saucers go on the second shelf."

As you set the table or do housework try simple addition with your child. "Two spoons plus one more spoon makes three spoons." One sock plus one sock makes two socks." "We had five oranges. You ate one. Now there are four oranges left. If you take 1 away from 5 how many are left?" Play card games such as "Fish" which use counting and numbers.

7. Learning the difference between real and seeming change

Often we change a thing in only *one* way. Little children may think we've made the thing completely different. Or they may think we've made it different in more than one way. They can't tell that it has changed in only one way.

Suppose you both have a muffin. You tear your muffin into bits. The pieces cover your whole plate. A young child might *think* you have more muffin to eat. It *looks like* more because it covers your whole plate.

Children are often fooled by what things *look like*. You may lay a string out straight or curvy. Either way, the string is just as long. The curled up string *looks* shorter. But it is just as long as the string when it is straight. You can help your child figure this out. Your child will learn when changes fool him or her into thinking the length or amount is different.

Some changes *do* cause differences. Boiling and frying and freezing transform foods. So does mashing. Foods may truly taste different *before* and *after* baking. Cooking games in this book will give you a chance to teach about *real* changes. Your child will learn about what kinds of changes occur. He or she will learn to notice them carefully.

8. Learning to use body parts together

Young children need to learn to use arm and leg and eye muscles together skillfully. They need to coordinate these muscles in games such as tricycle riding or skipping or jumping over a box. A preschooler who can use eyes and legs together will be better prepared to learn how to look carefully and then cross the street safely. When children coordinate body parts in hitting, rolling, kicking and throwing a ball they can feel good about themselves. They feel their bodies are working well.

When children learn to use fingers and hands and eyes together smoothly they have a good chance to —

- eat with forks and spoons without much mess
- drink without spilling
- clean up and put away toys and play materials neatly
- dress themselves using buttons and zippers correctly
- put away grocery packages and cans carefully
- learn how to print letters and numerals

- play games such as: stringing beads, or threading a shoe lace through punched holes in a cardboard picture, or building block towers
- prepare simple snacks, such as spreading peanut butter on a cracker
- start collections and arrange them (such as stamps or rocks or bugs or postcards)
- use blunt scissors to cut out interesting pictures to collect or to paste in a homemade book

9. Learning to reason

To succeed in school, a child needs to learn how to think and give reasons. Your child needs your help in learning *how* to think, *how* to find reasons in order to solve problems. Games in this book will give you a chance to help your child think in a more organized way.

Good reasoning helps family life run more smoothly. Help your child use "if-then" and "because" in thinking about what to do and why. Here is an example of good thinking skills a child can learn to use.

"My wagon can't fit through the door *because* the wagon is too fat and wide. *If* I turn my wagon on its side, *then* it will be skinny enough to fit through the door."

10. Learning to use imagination

A rich imagination helps make life more interesting. A rich imagination is a help to artists, musicians, and actors. Imagination makes us more interesting as friends. You can help your child think more creatively and develop his or her imagination. You can pretend-play with your children. For example, while your child

rides a tricycle, pretend it is a car and that you are sell-
ing gasoline at a gas station. Or, while taking out the
laundry, play a "what if" game. "What if a baby bunny
is hiding in all these towels and clothes. What should we
do?"

Encourage your children when they play pretend
games that are safe. Help them by providing some
"props" for their games. A bedspread thrown over a card
table can make a cave or a house or a garage for children
with lively imaginations.

Provide old clothes and boxes so your child can
pretend to play different people — a mama, a father, a
repair or salesperson, a firefighter, or a bus driver.

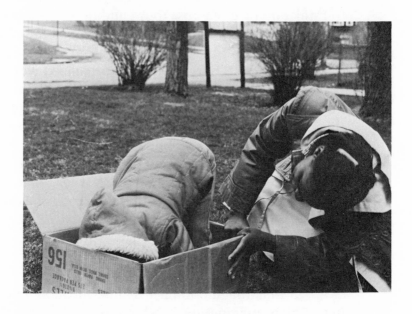

11. Learning language and using books

Language is a great power. You are an especially
important person in giving the gift of this great power to

your child. Most of the games in this book will help your child learn language. Your child will learn more and more words to use and questions to ask. He or she will learn to listen to what you say and learn to answer you correctly.

Talk about things that happen. Help your child learn to use words to describe what *has* happened or what *will* happen. Have your child describe what went on in play or what the child is wishing or feeling.

Talk a lot with your child about what you are both doing during the day. Help your child *listen* for the sounds of words. Play the "sounds" game in this book.

Keep language a loving activity in your family. Suppose a child hears harsh words often. That child may get turned off from liking language. That child may learn to use tough, harsh words that are not pleasant for you.

Learning to read is based on good listening and talking skills. Learning to read is also based on a good memory and on having lots of experiences. Help your child *look* carefully, *listen* carefully and *remember* well. This will boost your child's chances of learning to read well in school.

Boost your child's listening skills by giving clear rules and requests. Be sure your children understand all your words so that they can try to do what you ask them.

Children need to learn how to remember the rules that parents have. If your child can *tell* you the rules you have, then chances are those rules will be remembered better. Instead of scolding, if your child comes to the dinner table with dirty hands, use language power. Say "Remember the rule about hands before we eat our meals. Tell me the *rule* about hands." The child who gets chances to practice remembering and saying rules is more likely to try to pay attention to those rules.

Go to your local library every week. You and your

child will find wonderful books for preschool age children. Your child will look forward to carrying home an armful of new books, with new pictures and new stories.

Encourage your child to sit and turn pages and tell you the stories in the picture books. Treat book time as a special family treat time. Help your child feel that books are special treasures. Book times should be pleasure times everyday for your child. Read to your child every day.

12. Learning social skills

Becoming sociable, happy, and emotionally secure is a basic learning task for children.

You are the key person in helping your child become emotionally healthy. You give your child large amounts of love and personal attention. You help your child feel that he or she is an important member of your family.

Your child needs to learn self-control. For example, children need to obey the rule about not playing with matches. They need to wait if dinner is served a bit late without getting very upset. They need to learn that they can *feel* jealous about a baby sister or brother but they must not hurt the baby. Preschoolers need their parents to teach them how to express and to handle emotions.

Give your child jobs that must be done, such as brushing teeth, cleaning up spills, putting away toys. *Show* your child what you expect. Ask politely: "Please put a fork next to each plate on the table." Praise or thank the child for a job well done. Children need to feel pride in themselves. They need to *feel* that they are important and capable members of your family.

Hugging, smiling and patting your child are gestures that show you love your child. You are helping your child build a good self-concept.

Children who feel good about themselves can use their emotional energy for learning about the world. They do not need to brood or fight or pester for attention. They feel self confident. Your generous loving builds a child's self-confidence in living and learning.

If your child acts scared or shy *don't* ridicule or shame him or her. Sometimes grown-ups are afraid too. Fear can be a help if it makes us more *careful* about hot stoves or traffic crossings or walking on escalator stairs.

You also help your child when you *talk about feelings*. Accept your child's right to have bad feelings as well as good feelings. You may refuse to accept bad *actions* from your children. But their feelings belong to them. They will be emotionally healthier because you give them the right to have many different kinds of feelings.

Talk with your children about what makes them happy or upset, giggly, or angry. Help your child express feelings in an acceptable way. Each child has a right to *feelings*, whether pleasant or mean, although children cannot be allowed to *act* mean or hurting to others. Read stories where animals or children express different feelings. Talk about your own feelings. It helps children to see how grownups try to cope when they are feeling tired or worried or grumpy. Parents can show how to find ways to calm down and use self-control even when feelings are upset.

You also help by teaching your child polite ways to behave with others. Your child will have more friends if he or she learns to ask for things politely. Suppose your child asks if he or she can play with Ann's toys. Suppose another child roughly grabs Ann's toys. Ann is more likely to enjoy your child than the other child who grabs.

You can help your child by teaching him or her how to solve conflicts. The social skills game at the end of this book shows how to do this. Children can learn

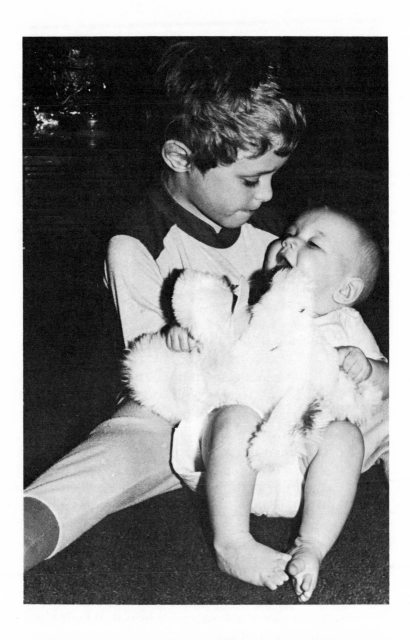

how to solve problems with others in socially positive
ways. You can encourage your child to think of different
ideas to work out a problem. If two children are fussing

with each other, encourage ideas that allow both persons to work out the problem. The aim is for both to feel OK.

It is hard for young children to take the point of view of *another* person. You will need to help your child a lot in building this and other social skills.

Tips for Getting the Most out of Learning Games

Keep learning games pleasant. Use smiles, hugs, and praise to keep a child working. Change your voice tones. Use a mystery voice or an excited voice. Keep the games interesting.

Dance up and down the learning ladder

When a game is too hard always think of an easier way to play it. Pretend you are dancing up and down a ladder of learning. When your child finds a game is too hard, dance down the ladder to lower rungs. Use fewer items. Give hints. Use favorite toys or bits of healthy food. For example, in the "Remembering what you saw" game, your child has to remember which cup you put something under. Let the child who guesses right get to eat a strip of green pepper or carrot. The game will be good for the tummy, good for memory, and good for the child's pride at being a successful learner.

When the game seems easy, then dance back up the learning ladder with your child. Make your questions harder. Use toys and objects that your child doesn't know very well yet.

Watch your child for *clues*. Then you will know when you need to dance up or down the learning ladder.

Children get discouraged when the learning game seems too difficult. Children get restless and fidgity if the games are too easy. If you are good at dancing the learning ladder with your child then you can keep your learning games not too easy and not too hard. Your child will be eager to learn with you.

When an idea is *difficult*, break it up into smaller parts for your child. Check out whether each step or part is understood. Then you can move on to the next part of the game.

Make a magic triangle

Why bother to keep your voice interesting? What's so important about using toys your child loves? By doing these things, you will make a magic triangle. *You, the child*, and *the toy* are the three magic parts of the triangle. The child will become very absorbed with the game.

By creating a magic triangle, you will increase your child's learning. He or she will be able to *stick with an activity* longer. This will make your child a better worker in school.

Use the real thing for younger ones

With a very young child, use *real* objects or foods or toys. Words or pictures alone are sometimes too hard for little children to work with. Be *sure* that your child knows well that a picture stands for a real object. Then you can use pictures.

The same-or-different games, for example, can be played with objects or pictures.

TLC: The special secret recipe for learning

Use your own home, your own neighborhood to help your child learn. As much as possible, turn daily chores and activities into opportunities for teaching. As you cook, repair, shop, visit, prepare, clean up, tend plants or pets, use your imagination. Find the learning games that can be played naturally in each situation. You will enjoy the challenge of finding the hidden learning games in everyday household routines. Your child will profit from your good ideas, your company and your conversations. You will be a special TLC parent — who provides tender loving care in a home that is a Total Learning Center.

Be a word giver

Always use *words* to help your child learn language that describes what is happening. Children need you to teach them the *names* of people, objects, actions, and feelings. Be a *word* giver. Give words about experiences. Learning is easier when we have words to explain what we are doing or seeing or feeling.

Enjoy your child

Above all, *enjoy* being your child's teacher. Catch your child doing well at learning. Use praise to let your child know when you are proud and pleased. Children love to hear their favorite teachers, their parents, tell them how well they are learning. Your encouragement will be like vitamins to nourish your child's self-esteem. Your enjoyment in working together at learning games will build healthy emotions as well as healthy positive attitudes toward learning.

Children learn by doing

Whenever a child is getting bored, try to get the child to be active in the game. Your child will enjoy *doing* all the actions called for by a space words game. Children learn well when they can move around and touch. Acting ideas out aids learning.

The water game is a good example of this. Children get pleasure from *playing with* as well as learning about water.

Play, play, play

For young children, play is the natural way to learn. As they play things happen. Colors blend. Clay gets dry. A sand pie falls to pieces. A wagon tips over.

As each event happens, the child can *learn*. Children learn about how wagons tip and clay dries out. They discover that they can change things. This leads to *What-if-I-change-this?* games. Then many children take the next step. They play a *What-if-I-do-this-next?* game. In this way, they find out what will happen if they change the way they are *using* something.

Children *at play* with each other also learn about social rules.

Arrange for *safe* and *happy* play experiences for your child — with toys and with other children.

Be a careful matchmaker

When you buy toys, choose carefully. Choose a toy that is just right for your child's stage of growing. Some toys will be too hard to use. A fifty-piece puzzle for a two-year-old will frustrate the child. Pieces may just get thrown around. It would be better to get a ten-piece puzzle.

Watch carefully *where* your child is at on the learning ladder. Try to *match* the games and toys you provide with what your child is *ready* to learn. Be a careful matchmaker!

When you make a game easier or harder so it fits your child, you are being a good matchmaker. This is one of the best talents a parent can have. Matchmaking is not easy. You can be proud of yourself when you dance up and down the learning ladder so well that your matchmaking is just right. Then games you play with your child will be *just* right to help learning.

Don't compare your child with others

Don't worry about what someone else's child did at this age. Plan learning games for *your* child. Children are all special. They do not learn things in exactly the same way or at the same age as other children. When you match up your games to *your* child, you are giving your child a wonderful gift. It's the gift of treating that child as a *one-of-a-kind child*.

One final note before you get into the games

None of the two dozen games in this book are for boys only or for girls only. But we didn't want to say *him or her* all the way through the book. So in some games we use *he, him, his*. In other games we use *she, her, hers*. No matter what pronoun is used, the game is for both boys and girls.

Playtime Learning Games for Young Children

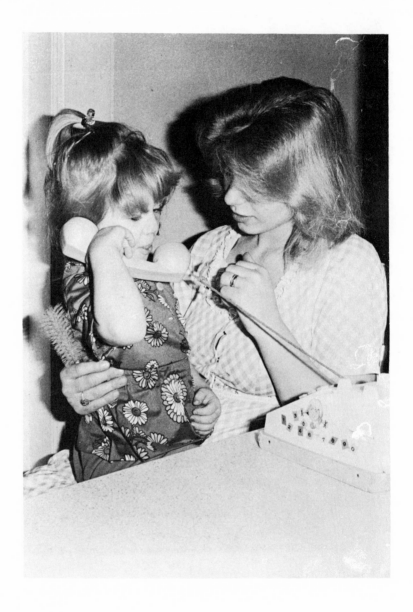

THE GAMES

1 People We Know

What you need

The names of some family members and friends whom your child knows

What you do

Help your child figure out how the people in her life are related. Talk about relatives and *how* they are all part of your family. If you can, show the child photos as you talk.

Ask your child to remember a certain uncle, for example. Can she describe the uncle? Can she remember which aunt goes with that uncle?

Use family words to help a child learn about cousins, nieces, nephews, grandfathers, and others. Maybe the child uses a word such as *Nana*. You may have to explain that *Nana* is her grandmother.

Find out if your child knows the names of friends and babysitters. Does she know the names of others in her life? Use words like *friends* and *neighbors* as you talk.

Other ways to play the game

When you are sure your child knows family names well, ask silly questions. Ask questions such as "Is John your *aunt*?" Such questions will usually make the child laugh. She will tell you John can't be an aunt. Then you ask her to remind you what kind of relative John is.

We call a relative by different kin names. The name we use depends on how we are related to the relative. For example, Sally may be your child's *cousin*. But she is your *niece*. If your child is an older preschooler, begin explaining this. Sally can be a cousin *and* a niece. A man can be a daddy and a truckdriver. The same person can belong to two different groups.

Be patient. It may take a long while for a child to understand kin relations. The differences are confusing to a young child.

You can help by pointing out many examples. Suzy, for example, is Bobby's sister. But Bobby isn't Suzy's *sister*. Bobby is her _____. Let the child fill in the kin name of brother. She will enjoy getting to know the words used to describe family and friends.

Purpose of the game

Families and friends are very important to children. Relatives help children feel secure about their place in the world. Children need to know about those who care for them and are close to them.

Your child learns that the same relative can be called by different names. The name people use depends on how they are related to the relative. Learning *who* uses *what* kin name helps a child begin to learn to take the speaker's point of view. Looking at family relations from *each* person's point of view helps a child relate to others. It's a good way for her to begin thinking of how *other* people see things.

2 Laundry Lists

What you need

A lot of dirty clothes to wash, to dry, and to put away

A place to wash clothes, such as a washing machine or tub

What you do

Sit down with your child. Explain that today is laundry day. Tell the child that you need help in *remembering* all the dirty clothes that may need to be washed. Ask the child to tell you something that may need washing. Write down each item the child says. You may want to draw a picture of each item.

If the child remembers socks and T-shirts, help him remember more. Say, "You remembered socks from our *feet* and shirts from our *tops*. Are there other clothes to wash from other parts of our bodies?"

When you both finish the list, look in the laundry. Check which things are there that the child guessed.

Let the child help you *sort* the dirty laundry into *light* colors and *dark* colors. Talk about what happens sometimes if we mix a white blouse and a dark red shirt in hot water.

Let the child help you fill up your washer and add soap. Let him put clothes into the washer one by one. Let him *name* each item for you. If the child can count, let him count how many socks you are washing. Count the other items being washed.

When the tub or washer is filled with water, let the child hold one dry sock and one wet one. Ask him to

tell you how they *feel*. Which one feels *heavier?* Can he tell you *why?*

Talk about the *sequence* of your actions. *First* you sort clothes. Next you load the washer. Then you fill in water. After that you add soap. You may add bleach or softener *later* or *last*. Use *time sequence* words as you work to help your child experience what these words mean.

Other ways to play the game

Include the child in drying and folding the clothes, too. The child can help sort dry clothes into piles of items that are the *same*. Or he can find the *little* underpants and the *big* underpants. He can fold sheets with you. Talk about getting *corners* even. Talking about *smoothing* and *folding*. Ask the child to find all the *pairs* of socks. Show how to match up a pair of socks. Teach the child to roll socks up in a neat ball.

Purpose of the game

This game will help a child feel useful. Doing laundry is a big help to the family.

Your child will learn the *order* in which you sort, wash, dry, and fold laundry.

Your child learns to make groups while arranging a pile of clean clothes that belongs to each person in the family.

Your child will learn about the *textures* of clothes. He'll learn how different kinds of clothes feel.

Your child will notice the *temperature* of water. It may be hot for washing and cool for rinsing.

Your child will feel the difference in the *weight* of wet and dry clothes.

Your child will learn to *compare* and match clothing and other laundry items.

You get to show your child that you enjoy his company. You are thankful for his help in your work. This makes a child feel loved and an important part of the family.

You praise your child as he *remembers* what needs to be washed. This encourages him to notice and remember things more exactly. Good noticing and remembering are important skills. They will be a big help to your child's success with school work.

3 How Many Things Can You Tell Me about This?

What you need

Almost any object or toy in the house or yard will do.

Start with things your child knows well. They should have a definite shape, use, and color. These might include a ball, box, key, pencil, washcloth, spoon, soap, rubber band, or piece of rope.

What you do

Ask your child to tell you all that he can about each object. Encourage your child. Say, "Good, you told me the *name* of this. You told me what it is *made* of. Now can you tell me something else about this?"

Hold the child's interest by hiding each object in your hands first. Then open your hands and ask, "Tell me about *this*!" Make your voice a "mystery" voice to get your child into the spirit of the game.

Other ways to play the game

Make this game easier by asking questions about the object:

- What do we call it?
- What does it do?
- How do people usually use it?
- What shape does it have?
- How big is it?

- What color is it? Could it be another color?
- How hard or soft or bumpy or smooth does it feel?
- Does it have points or corners?
- What other kinds are there?

Be sure to give your child plenty of time to answer you. Appreciate your child's answer.

Make this game harder by urging the child to think of *more* ways to describe the object.

Purpose of the game

Your child learns to think about things more carefully.

Your child learns that naming an object is only one way to describe it. There are many *more* ways to describe an object. Different objects belong in different groups, such as square, or blue or soft.

Your child learns words and ideas such as these:

- it has four corners
- it feels rubbery
- it is hard
- you can fold it
- you can put something in it
- round
- you can roll it
- it feels bumpy
- slippery
- you eat with it

4 Water Games

What you need

A bathtub

A safe stool so your child can climb up and reach the kitchen sink

A deep plastic tup on a tile floor or outdoors

Water toys—

- a funnel
- aluminum foil pans
- an old coffee pot
- an empty margarine bowl
- plastic shampoo bottles
- big and little plastic cups
- sieve or strainer
- drinking straw
- spoons
- eggbeater
- corks

Include some empty juice cans of different sizes. One should have a small drip hole in the bottom. Another should have a hole in the cardboard side of the can. Juice cans can be used for pouring, for dripping, for squirting. Make sure none of the toys have edges that could cut. They should be toys that won't break.

Add vegetable coloring to the water if you wish.

What you do

Let the child explore the water. The child will find out how water works by pouring from cups to pots to bottles to cans to strainer. He will find out what *leaks*

and what *drips*. He will learn what containers hold
more water and *less* water. Use these words with your
child.

Get the child to tell you what he has tried to do
while playing. Ask him what he is finding out about
water.

Talk about which is easier to pour from — a cup
with a pouring lip or a regular cup? Can the child explain why?

Make sure the child has lots of time to enjoy the
water toys. Give him time to find out how water flows,
drips, squirts, pours, and spills. Let him make bubbles
with an egg beater, whisk, or soda straw.

Other ways to play the game

Can the child find ways to make floating toys
sink? Give the child some old keys or bottle caps or
spoons. Let him put these on floating pans or cups. Ask
your child how many spoons he needs to sink an aluminum pie pan. Ask how much it takes to sink the margarine tub.

Try to get your child to talk about what is happening. Floating and sinking are hard ideas to understand. Respect your child's way of explaining what
causes something to sink.

Another game involves making a floating toy
move in the water. Tell the child not to touch the toy
with his hands. Ask if he can move the toy without
touching it.

Encourage the child to try to solve this problem.
The child might make waves in the water. He might
blow on the floating toy. Praise your child for try-

ing hard to think of ways to make the floating toy sail.

Even very young children enjoy water play at bath time. Use bathtub time as a fun let's-get-clean time. But also provide floating and sinking toys. Provide bubble bath at times. These things will help your child learn about water.

Many children love to help wash dishes. Use plastic plates, so your child can help soap and rinse and dry dishes. The child will learn words such as *slippery, still soapy*, and *we need to rinse again*.

Show your child how important water is in the world. Show him where water is found — in rain, rivers, lakes, and oceans. Show him dew on grass in early morning. Watch the dew go away as the sun comes out. A little water left in a dish will evaporate also.

Tell the child that water is very wonderful. We need to drink it when we are thirsty. We need water to get clean. We need water to flush our toilets. Talk about *all* the ways we use water. Show your child how a plant droops if it is dry. Let your child help water your house plants carefully.

A child needs to learn about the world he lives in. Give your child many chances to play with sand or mud or water. This helps him learn about how substances work. Stay with the child, so he will be safe. Your being there gives the child a chance to talk about what he is learning.

Even when the child's actions seem foolish to you, don't laugh at him. For example, he may pour water through the tiny end of a funnel. Let the child discover alone which end works best. Ask, "Which end is best for helping you not to spill water as you pour?" "How can you use a funnel to get water from a big pot into a shampoo bottle?"

Purpose of the game

Your child learns about the world she lives in.

Your child learns about how substances work.

Your child learns to share his discoveries with others.

Children have a lot of curiosity. This drives them to keep on trying to find out how things work. Water is very good for helping children spend a *long* time playing and discovering. The child learns to stick with a learning experience.

Your child gets to try out her *own* ideas with water toys. She thinks, "I can learn on my own. I can figure out how to pour and how to make bubbles."

Sometimes the best way we can help a child with a learning game is to *arrange* toys and safe exploring experiences. Then children can be *active* learners. They can find out "what happens if." This kind of learning is very good. We remember better when we learn by discovering things through our own efforts.

5 Guessing Differences: A Sentence Completion Game

What you need

A list of sentences about habits well-known to your child

What you do

Tell your child you are both going to play a game. You will start saying something. The child will have to *guess* how to finish what you say. Give an easy example:

We touch with our *fingers*. We hear with our _____.

Your blanket feels *soft*. A rock feels _____.

Raise your voice on words like *fingers* and *soft*. These words give hints to the child. They tell your child the kind of answer you expect.

Other ways to play the game

If the child has trouble, fill in the missing word. Then repeat the whole sentence. After this, give your child a chance to say the missing word.

Make up some funny sentences to keep the child interested:

We stand on our feet. We sit on our _____.

Here are more sentences. Some are easy. Some are hard. Always try the ones that are easy first with a younger child.

Dogs say *bow wow*. Cats say _____.

We drink with a *cup*. We eat with a _____.

A hat goes on your *head*. Shoes go on your _____.

A baby dog is a *puppy*. A baby cat is a _____.

We see with our *eyes*. We smell with our _____.

We sleep in the *night*. We wake up in the _____.

We sit *down*. We stand _____.

A doctor can fix a hurt in your *tummy*. A dentist can fix a hurt in your _____.

We cry when we are *sad*. We smile when we are _____.

A fly says *buzz-buzz*. A bird says _____.

We eat breakfast in the *morning*. We eat supper at _____.

A bunny has a *short* tail. A horse has a _____.

A red traffic light means *stop*. A green light means _____.

Plates are *clean* before a meal. They are _____ after a meal.

A refrigerator feels *cold*. A stove feels _____.

A baby *creeps* and *crawls*. A big child like you can _____.

A bed is for sleeping. A chair is for _____.

To close a box, put the top *on*. To open a box, take the top _____.

A mouse *squeaks*. A lion _____.

When it rains, it is *wet*. When there is *no* rain, it is _____.

A mouse is *little*. An elephant is _____.

A flower smells *sweet*. Garbage smells _____.

If just using words is too hard for your child, wait a while. Meanwhile, point out differences as she plays or helps with jobs in the house. Help her notice that soup is *hot*, but ice cream is *cold*. Have her listen to birds *singing* and crickets *chirping*. This practice will prepare her for playing the differences game. She may remember the differences you talked about and showed her. Then she can complete the sentences with the right words.

Purpose of the game

Your child learns to listen carefully.

Your child learns to make good guesses about *how* things are *different*.

Your child learns to pay attention to you as a teacher.

6 Egg Carton Color Cups

What you need

> An egg carton made of white material
> Magic markers or colored crayons
> Some thin sheets of colored paper
> A basket or bowl

What you do

Have the child choose a colored marker and *name* the color. Let the child color inside one of the egg carton cups. She should color until the color is easy to see.

Have the child choose another colored marker. Let her color another cup. Be sure the child knows the name of each color she chooses and uses. Each egg cup will be colored a different color.

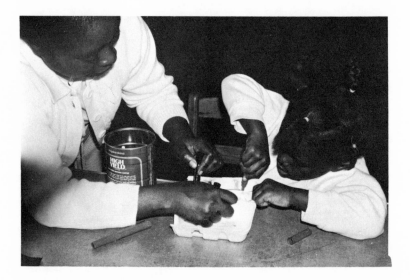

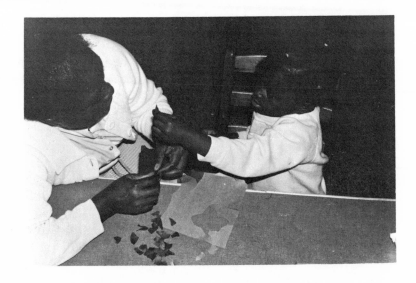

Ask the child to tear into strips each sheet of colored paper. Then she can tear the strips into tiny bits. Mix all the paper bits together in a bowl.

Let the child fish out a bit of colored paper from

the bowl. Can she tell you the name of the color? Can she find which color cup matches the bit of paper?

This game is finished when each egg carton cup is filled with paper bits of the *same* color as the cup.

Other ways to play the game

If your child is not very sure of colors, use only three or four colors. Start with red, green and black, perhaps. Be sure you name each color often. The child can color three egg cups with each of the three colors. This gives the child a chance to match colors at an easier level.

When the child is secure with a few easy color names, add more colors. Here are some more difficult shades and colors:

- turquoise (blue-green)
- lemon yellow
- gray
- orange

- rose
- tan
- violet
- brown

If the child learns more and more of these harder color names, say, "You sure are learning the names for many *different* colors. I am really proud of how many colors you are learning."

If the child is really sure at this game, sometimes try a trick. The child might pick up a bit of orange paper. You could then ask, "That goes in the rose egg cup, doesn't it?" Your child will enjoy catching you making a mistake. Children enjoy playing "teacher." They like telling adults the right answer.

You can also help your child learn colors by mixing poster paints or using water color sets. Then you will be able to extend your child's awareness of color mixing.

Yellow and red make orange. Yellow and blue make green.

Build on your child's new awareness of color. How many places can she find red in her room or in the kitchen? Can he find any blue on his clothes today? What colors can your child find in a plaid blanket or in argyle socks?

Purpose of the game

Your child learns color names.

Your child learns to notice and match different colors.

Fingers get practice in tearing colored papers into tiny bits and in holding crayons well while coloring.

7 Stories and Songs

What you need

Some you-and-me time when you can just talk with your child.

Story books for preschoolers (your local library should have plenty of these)

Songs you know how to sing

Large colorful interesting pictures (cut them out of old magazines. Keep them in an envelope or folder)

Stories about your life that you can tell to a child

Some planning time for talking with your child about what you *plan* to do

What you do

Encourage your child to talk with you. Ask your child to tell you about his experiences. Ask about games, visits, friends, day care, baby sitters, and other experiences. Listen carefully to your child. Let him feel that what he says is important.

Listen carefully to your child's questions. Take time to help him think through to answers.

Take your child to the library. Choose books together. Choose animal stories with simple, bright-colored pictures. Choose other books your child likes.

Read to your child every day. Change your voice from low to high. Speak softly, then loudly. Keep the story interesting so the child will wish he or she could read it too. Read or tell favorite stories over and over. Your child wants to hear familiar stories that he recognizes and loves and knows well.

Ask your child to point to parts in picture books. Say, "Show me the lion's eyes, legs, paws . . ."

Ask questions about the stories, such as:

Why was it foolish (silly) for the little pig to build a house out of straw? ("Three Little Pigs")

How did the bears know that Goldilocks had been eating their cereal? ("Goldilocks & the Three Bears")

Why did the baby bird have to *walk* down the tree to go look for his mother? ("Are You My Mother?")

Why is the big bad wolf wearing Grandmother's cap? ("Little Red Riding Hood").

Sing with your child. Here are 12 songs young children love to sing.

1. *Old MacDonald had a farm* (your child will enjoy making all the animal noises)

2. *Do the hokey pokey*

3. *If you're happy and you know it clap your hands*

4. *The farmer in the dell*

5. *London bridges falling down, my fair lady*

6. *Ring around a rosy*

7. *Eentsy beentsy spider climbed up the water spout*

8. *Where is thumbkin?*

9. *Hush little baby*, don't say a word; Mama's gonna buy you a mockingbird

10. *Brother John (Frere Jacques)*

11. *Row, row, row your boat*

12. *Jingle bells*

Show you child your cut-out pictures. Ask him to describe what is going on in the picture. Say, "Tell me all about this picture?"

A younger child may not be able to tell much. He may say *who* is there or *what* is there.

Four-, five-, and six-year-olds, can tell you more. They can describe what is happening. They may tell what has happened already and what will happen next. They may be able to tell what the people in the picture are feeling.

Praise your child for telling you so many things about the picture. Act very interested in what the child says.

Tell your child stories from your own life. Talk about your family, how you lived, what you liked to play with, your friends, what chores you used to do, what happened to you on special holidays and celebrations.

Tell your child stories about when she or he was a little baby and then a bigger baby. Talk about how much you needed to feed the baby and how the baby gave you so much happiness with early coos and smiles and first steps and first words. Snuggle your child as you tell the

"story of when you were a baby." Talk about how much you loved the child as a baby and as a toddler and now as a child beginning to learn so much that she or he will soon be ready for school.

Other ways to play the game

Read longer stories to older children; ask them more questions.

Let younger children *act out* the stories. If a bunny in the story is hopping, a two-year-old may want to hop too.

Give story stems to older children. A story stem is half a story. Let the children make up the ending.

Have the child put your cut out pictures in order. Or, read a comic strip to your child. Then cut up the strip into the separate pictures. Say, "Put the pictures in order so they tell a story."

Plan singing times. Choose special songs for when you are getting your child ready for sleep. Choose songs for walking with in rhythm along a street. Use melodies such as "This is the way we wash our clothes" and change the words to fit the household jobs you are doing with your child's help.

Purpose of the game

These games help your child use language. Giving your child the power to use language well is a priceless gift.

Your child learns to love books and understand stories. He learns to "read" pictures. This will give a big boost to his success in school.

Your child is encouraged to express ideas. Children do this when "reading" pictures to you or when answering your questions. This helps them to think more. It increases their language skills.

Songs make language learning easier. Songs especially help shy and slow-to-talk children to feel more able to use language.

We all need to share our ideas, feelings, and experiences. Language games help your child do this.

8 Food Names

What you need

Take your child along when you go shopping in the supermarket.

What you do

Point out foods and name each food. Be sure to show your child different —

- vegetables
- meats
- fruits
- cheeses
- fish

- breads
- cereals
- juices
- produce
- and other foods

Tell your child you want to see how many foods she can name. Point to a food and ask, "What food is that one?" See how many different food names the child knows. See if she can tell what a food is by the picture on the label. Carrots, for example, are easier to recognize in a plastic bag. They are harder to recognize in a can or a frozen vegetable box. The can or box only shows a picture of carrots. The plastic bag lets your child see the actual food.

Act happy when your child names a food correctly. Praise your child for naming foods from pictures on labels.

If your child answers "Meat!" when you point to ham, say, "Yes, these are *all* meats. But this meat right here has a special name. This one is called ham. This other meat [point to it] is called hamburger."

When you are buying some items let your child

learn to *make choices.* For example, you can hold up 2 or 3 boxes of whole grain non-sugared cereal, name them, and ask, "Which one shall we buy?" The child gets to name the cereal of his choice. You have given choices from nutritious cereals, not junk food. Your child will feel proud to choose and select some foods. Help a child notice which grapefruit or other produce is fresh. The fresh fruit has a smooth skin. You can sharpen your child's noticing skills. Such visual noticing skills will help your child in learning to see small differences in written letters and words.

Other ways to play the game

After shopping, let your child help you arrange food on the shelves at home. The child can find cans of vegetables. She can put them together in one place on a shelf.

Can your child find all the *salad* items? Have her bring the lettuce, tomatoes, celery, cucumbers, and radishes to the refrigerator.

Talk to your child about which foods must be kept cold. Explain that fresh meat can spoil if left on a shelf. Fresh milk will turn sour unless it is kept cold. Ask your child to name foods which stay fresh on a shelf. These could include spaghetti, canned foods, and peanut butter. Can your child name foods that must be kept cold to keep fresh?

Purpose of the game

Your child will learn the names of many foods.
Your child will begin to learn about food groups.

She may learn that rolls, buns, and muffins are all *breads*. Bread is a big food group. So is meat. So is fruit. The child learns the names for these big food groups. She learns the names of each food *inside* each food group.

Some food groups are very good for your health. They keep children strong and well. This game can help your child understand more about foods. She'll learn where they are found, how they are stored, and to which groups they belong. She'll learn which are good for growing up healthy.

9 First Place–Last Place

What you need

Small objects such as toothpicks, juice cans, checkers, bottle caps, or small blocks

What you do

You and your child line up the objects in a long row.

Ask your child to show you the *first* car of your pretend train.

Ask your child to point to the *last* car of the train.

It doesn't matter which end of the train the child chooses for the front. Just make sure the other end has the *last* car.

Other ways to play the game

Make the train longer or shorter. The child needs to learn that *first* and *last* are places that don't depend on how many objects are present.

If the game is too hard, point out the front car, the *first* car. Do this by piling up three black checkers or bottle caps for an engine. Put two red checkers for the *last* car — the caboose. Tell your child that the engine is first in line. The caboose comes at the end of the train. It is the *last* car.

Line up your train so that there are an uneven number of cars. Ask your child to find the middle car of the train.

If this is too hard, let the child take away the first

car. You take away the last car. Then the child takes away the *second* car. You take away the *next-to-last* car. Each of you take away a car at the same time until one car is left. This car is the *middle* car. Have your child count the cars he took away. You count the cars you took from your end. Let him see that you have the same number of cars. Say, "The middle car has the same number of cars on each side of it."

When you walk with your child, point to the *first* house on the block. See if your child can find the *last* house on the block. Look for the middle house on the block. There may be two middle houses if there is an even number of houses. Ask your child to tell you why this is so.

Let your child line up different things in the house. He may line up clothespins, or toy animals or cars. Ask, "Which one is first in line? Which is in the middle? Which is last?"

Put the train cars in a circle. Can there be a first and last car now? The train must have a beginning and end to have a first and last car.

Purpose of the game

Your child learns the names for places in a line or row. This will help the child in school. He will understand when a teacher asks children to line up. A teacher may expect the children to understand words like *first place* and *last place*. The child may need to understand *second place* or *next-to-last place* or *middle place*.

Your child learns to line up his belongings more carefully and neatly.

10 Sounds Game

What you need

Lots of easy words the child knows already

What you do

Say a word. Then ask the child to tell what sound it starts or ends with. Ask what sound is in the middle of the word:

What sound does _____ start with?

What sound does _____ end with?

What sound do you hear in the middle of this word?

Here are some words you could use:

Start sounds	*End sounds*	*Middle sounds*
it	ice	heavy
cat	soup	speak
foot	brush	spool
too	hand	puppy
hair	bell	fishing
*television	cake	belly
mother	ham	table
beans	leaf	horse
grits	balloon	and so on
friend	bus	
rake	choo-choo	
shoe	supermarket	
open	and so on	
jump		
*delicious		
nose		
even		
*lollypop		
and so on		

*Say to your child, "It's a long word. Be careful."

Other ways to play the game

To make the game harder, use longer words. Use some words where there are two or more clear middle sounds. For example, ma*r*ket has an "r" and "k" sound in the middle.

Ask your child to be a *copy cat*. You say a word that *starts* with a sound. Your child has to say a different word that starts with the *same* sound.

If you say *table*, ask your child to say a word that starts with the same sound as your word. Be sure you say the "t" in *table* very clearly. Then the child will be able to *copy* your sound. Accept any words the child says that start with your "t" sound.

If the child has trouble, you can give a hint. *Point* to something that begins with a "t." Point to a toe or television or toy truck. If you had said *boat*, you could point to a bag or banana or ball or bowl.

Smile and praise your child for correct guesses. Then ask your child to copy cat on *ending* sounds. If you said *bread*, the child could say be*d* or re*d*.

Make a list of the words your child uses to go with each sound. She'll be proud to see how many words she thought of.

Rhyming is another way to play the sounds game. Explain to your child about rhymes: Two words rhyme if they sound alike. They need *ending* sounds that are the *same*. Give your child some examples:

fish-wish-dish	spot-hot-pot	rose-nose-blows
cat-sat-bat	beat-seat-feet	dog-hog-log
squash-wash	boat-note-coat	nice-rice-ice

Have fun with rhymes together. Words that end in -*and* are easy to do: hand, band, land, sand. Words with -*an* are easy to rhyme: an, man, can, ran, van,

Dan, pan. Words with *-at* are easy to rhyme: at, cat, bat, hat, rat.

Accept nonsense rhymes if the child has found the right sound but there is no such word A child shows imagination by making up a silly or nonsense rhyme to snuggle, such as "wuggle" or "tuggle!" Dr. Seuss books such as *The Cat in the Hat* series are marvelous for learning real and imaginary rhymes.

Purpose of the game

Your child learns to recognize beginning, ending, and middle sounds of words.

Your child becomes more skillful at *listening* to words.

Your child learns to make rhymes and have fun with rhymes.

11 How Else Could You Use This Toy? An Imagination Game

What you need

Choose some toys and objects your child knows well. Find items that interest your child. Then the child will want to try hard to find new ways to use the item. Here are some ideas for toys and objects to use:

- a paper bag
- a large cotton handkerchief
- a ball
- a box with a top
- an empty plastic detergent bottle
- wooden basting spoons
- an empty thread spool
- two forks
- a long piece of string

What you do

Tell your child that a paper bag can do many things. Some of these things everyone knows about. Ask, "What are some things you have seen Mr. Bag do?"

Your child may answer, "Carry food."

Then say, "Now let's try to think of lots of other things Mr. Bag can do. May we'll find secret things that only we know about. Let's think hard. As soon as you think of something, tell me!"

Do something like this for each item. As your child gives ideas, praise him. Say, "Yes, that is a good thing you could do with Mr. Bag. Now tell me another thing. Think of another way you could use the bag."

Don't be in a hurry to switch to a new object. Give your child a chance to use his imagination. Encourage your child to keep thinking up new uses for the toys you choose. Admire your child when he gives an interesting or creative idea. Laugh with him when he gives an idea he thinks is funny.

Other ways to play the game

You may enjoy taking turns with your child. First the child thinks up a different way to use the item. Then it is *your* turn to be creative. Think up some funny ways to use everyday objects. For example, you could hold two forks by the handles. Hold them straight up and down on the table. Pretend that the fork tines are toes and that the two forks are dancing partners.

Purpose of the game

This game will help wake up your child's imagination. Your child will begin to value thinking up interesting ideas.

Your child will enjoy a good time *socially*. You are both playing the game together. And you are really appreciating the child's good ideas.

12 Where Will My Doggie Sit? A Space Words Game

What you need

A small toy chair or couch
A toy truck and car
A toy animal
A box that is not very deep

What you do

Put the toy furniture and cars into the box. Sit on the floor with your child. Explain to your child that you will play a pretend game with a toy doggie: "This little dog just cannot make up his mind. First he wants to sit *on* the chair. Can you put the dog *on* the chair? Very good. Thank you for helping the dog to get up *on* the chair.

"Now the dog wants to jump *down* from the chair. Please help him jump *down*. Thank you!

"Now that dog just decided he wants to go *behind* the chair. Please walk the dog to a place *behind* the chair. Good! You are really a big help to the doggie.

"Well, that dog changed his mind again. Now he wants to sit *next* to the chair, *beside* the chair. Good. You helped him sit *next* to the chair.

"The dog is feeling sleepy. He wants to sleep *under* the chair. Please help him get *under* the chair.

"Oh, oh!" That dog just changed his mind again! Now he wants to go *under* the truck. Good, you put him under the truck. But that is not such a safe place for a dog. Maybe you can help him jump up *into* the truck. Now you can drive the truck all around *inside* the box.

"First, drive the truck in front of the chair. OK, now let's see you drive the truck *behind* the chair. Now can you pull up and park your truck right *beside* the chair? Good for you.

"Please help the doggie get down from the truck. Walk him around the truck.

"Now the dog wants to see if there is anything to eat in a *corner* of the box. Good. You found him one corner. Walk him to the next corner. Fine. How about a walk to another corner to look for food. Oh, you are right. There is *one more* corner to walk to. The box has four corners. Just like our room has four corners. See?

"I believe that doggie wants to do a silly thing. He wants to sit on the bottom side, the *underside* of the chair. Can you think of a way he could do that? Yes, you can turn the chair *upside down*. Now your doggie can sit on the underside of the chair.

Maybe your dog would like to jump very high right *outside* this box. Hooray. You jumped him right outside of his box. Now turn the whole box upside down. Let doggie pretend the box is a platform. He can stand on top and take a bow.

"You have been a good helper in our pretend game with the little dog."

Other ways to play the game

If this game is too hard with toys, let your child go to all the different places. Right in your home ask your child to get *on* a step or get *into* a box. Ask him to get *behind* a couch, *under* a table, go *around* a chair.

The child can walk from one corner of the room to the next one. He can count all four corners in turn. The child can put one hand *on top of* a table, then *under* a table. He can find the *top* of his head, the *top* of his shoes, the *bottom* of his feet. Help him by saying the place words as the child carries out all these actions.

Purpose of the game

Your child will learn the *names* of places. Your child will get practice in listening and following directions.

13 The Feely Box

What you need

A shoe box or any box with a top that is deep enough to put toys inside (Make a hole in the top big enough to allow the child to reach in and take out toys.)

What you do

Put objects in the box that the child knows really well. Here are some objects you might use:

- a piece of an old towel
- a piece of rope
- a cotton ball
- an empty juice can
- a piece of nylon mesh for scrubbing pots
- a shoe lace
- a small sponge
- a marble
- a comb
- a piece of fake fur
- a large button
- a small pencil
- a small rock
- a toothbrush
- a teaspoon
- a piece of soap
- a toy car
- a piece of chalk
- a bottle top

Have your child reach into the Feely Box. Tell her not to look, just feel. Get her to talk about what she

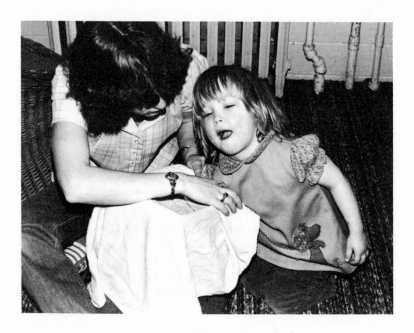

feels. The child should *guess* what the item is. Ask the child, "*How* can you tell? What do you feel that helps you guess?"

Let the child take out the toy. Check if the guess was correct. If the child named the item correctly, then she can leave this item out. If she did not guess correctly, put the item back in the box. The child will be more likely to guess that item correctly later on.

The game is over when all the items are out on the table. Praise your child for mentioning shape words, for talking about the smoothness or bumpiness of the items. Praise your child for being a good *detective*. The child is learning to *feel* clues with hands. These clues are signs to tell us what the item may be.

Use *words* to describe how *hard* stone feels or how *scratchy* nylon net feels. Talk about how *bristly* a

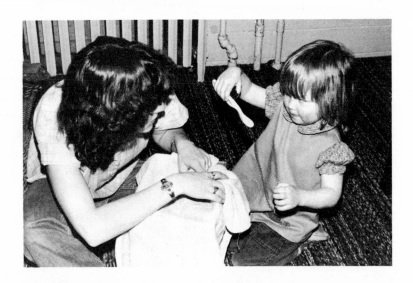

brush feels, how *sharp* a pencil point feels. Say that the piece of terry cloth towel feels *bumpy* and *soft*.

Other ways to play the game

For a very young child, put only three items in the Feely Box. Be sure the child knows each item well. At first, choose three things that are *very* different. These might be a ball, a brush, and a piece of string.

As the child finds the game easier, add more items.

Several children in a family may want to play this game. Let each one have a *turn*. Talk about how we take turns. Praise the children for patiently waiting their turn.

If a child has a very hard time guessing correctly *just* by feeling, then do this: Put a few items in the Feely Box. Put those same kind of items on the table. Seeing the kind of object that her hand is feeling, will give your child a big hint. Ask the child, "Do you feel something in the box that's like one of these things you see on the table? How can you tell it's the same?"

If the Feely Box game becomes too easy, you can always make guessing harder. Put objects in the box that the child doesn't know well. Try an eye dropper, a thimble, a bottle opener, a piece of elastic. Use a toy jack, a dry lima bean, a cereal box top, a hair pin, a belt buckle, a piece of celery, or an old sock.

Purpose of the game

School children are asked to describe things they have seen or felt or done. This game will encourage the skill of describing things.

Your child learns to *pay attention* to small hints and clues in order to make good guesses.

The child who plays the game with items in the Feely Box *and* out on the table, learns to *match* what is seen with what is felt.

Language grows as you help your child find words to *tell* you what she is feeling in the Feely Box.

14   A What, Where, When, How, Why Game

What you need

Many questions about places, people, and activities your child knows well

What you do

Help your child learn to answer questions clearly and correctly.

Help your child learn to ask questions that make sense.

Help your child learn to think hard about experiences.

Ask questions that start with the five question words. Here are some examples:

What   What street do we live on?
         What do we cook soup in?
         What color is grass?
         What does a mommy do? What does a daddy do?

Where   Where would we go to find a bus?
         Where would you go to see an elephant?
         Where are some swings?
         Where can you buy a hamburger?
         Where can you find a bowl for your cereal?

When   When do we eat breakfast?
         When do we get our clothes on and get dressed?
         When do you see the streets all wet?
         When do you need to help set the table?

Add in a loving *when* question: "When do I need to give you a hug and a kiss? Right now!" This surprise

question and loving hug will help your child *enjoy* playing learning games with you.

How   How does a puppy dog show you that he is
        happy?

        How can you reach a toy that rolls under the
        couch?

        How do we make toast?

        How do you brush your teeth?

        How do you make a sand pie?

        How do you play (marbles, tag, cowboy or any
        game the child plays)?

        How can you keep your feet dry if there are
        wet snow or rain puddles outside?

        How can you paint without getting your
        clothes messy?

        How can you stay warm outside in the winter
        time?

        How do you make a peanut butter sandwich?

        How does a cat drink milk?

How questions help a child think and reason in
an orderly way. For example, How do we make a bed?
First, we smooth the sheets. Then we put on the blanket.
After that we put the bedspread on top. Then we
smooth it all around.

Why   Why do we drink water?

        Why do we need a sink?

        Why do we have feet?

        Why do you need two children to make the
        teeter-totter go?

        Why do babies cry?

        Why do we wash dishes after we finish eating?

        Why does your shirt need buttons?

        Why do we need to look carefully in both
        directions before we cross the street?

Why shouldn't we put our glass of milk down on its side on the table?

Other ways to play the game

Answering *why* questions helps a child improve reasoning skills. But *why* questions will be hard for very young children. They may first answer, "Because." You can give hints to help a young child learn to reason better. You might say, "I wonder why we need feet. Do we need feet to see with or to listen with? No? Oh, then why *do* we need feet? What can we do with our feet? Yes, you are right. We can *walk* with feet. Now tell me again — *why* do we need feet?"

Giving hints makes it easier for a child to understand what *kind* of answer you expect.

For the older child, expect longer answers. Urge the child to explain more to you.

Let the child ask you *what, where, when, how,* and *why* questions. This gives you a chance to see how well he uses such questions. Be patient in answering children's questions. Children learn language best by asking questions and talking *with* grownups. Talk at meal times. Let your child talk to others as the family eats together.

Ask questions that will help your child make good guesses. During the course of conversations with your child or while doing your work as your child keeps you company, ask the child what she thinks has happened or will happen if she heard or saw or felt or smelled certain things. You can always ask the child how she figured that out or why she thinks that an event happened the way she explained it.

- If you were helping me with the dishes and you noticed your sleeve was soaking wet, what do you think would have happened?
- If we found a tiny baby bird on the ground and it could not fly, what do you think must have happened?
- If we forget to button your coat on a very windy day and you go outside, what do you think might happen?
- If you are building with your blocks and try to put a very big block on top of a very little block, what do you think might happen?
- If I make toast for you and it looks all black and stiff, what do you suppose has happened?
- If you hear a dripping sound in the bathroom or kitchen, what might we have forgotten to do?
- If we call someone on the telephone and we hear short beeps sounding in our ear, what do you suppose our friend is doing?

Purpose of the game

Your child learns to reason and think better.

Your child learns to make good guesses about what *has* happened or *will* happen.

A child who answers well shows that he is learning to understand what a question means.

Your child learns to think up good answers that fit well.

Your child will feel self-confidence that she can tell you about something she knows how to do or that she knows about.

15 Cooking Eggs: How Materials Change

What you need

A meal when you are cooking eggs

What you do

When you cook foods they *change* in firmness, texture, and taste. Show this to your child as you prepare eggs in different ways.

Boiled eggs. Boil two eggs. Take one out after three minutes. Tell your child this one was heated only a *short* time. We'll soon see what it looks like. Take the other egg out after 10 minutes. Say that this one was heated a *long* time. I wonder what *it* looks like.

Crack open the soft egg. You may want the child to scoop the egg out of the shell. She may also help you pick off or peel the shell of the hard egg.

Let your child taste both eggs. Then she can choose which one she'll eat and which one you'll eat.

Talk to the child about how more and more cooking *changes* the stuff inside the egg. Ask your child to tell you what the difference in taste is like.

Poached eggs. Show your child a raw egg. Teach her to crack an egg *carefully* and let the yolk and white slip into a bowl.

Boil some water. Point out to the child how the water *changes* as it gets hotter and hotter. Bubbles come. The water *boils*. *Steam* starts to form as the water boils. Turn your heat low.

Now let your child pour the raw egg carefully into the boiling water. Watch the egg poach. The boiling water *changes* the raw egg.

Have your child *talk* about the changes she sees as the egg gets poached. How does the poached egg taste? Why do we need a piece of toast with a poached egg?

Omelet or scrambled egg. Let your child break a raw egg carefully into a bowl. The child can learn to whip the egg with a fork. Point out how *foamy* the beaten egg looks. How else has it changed? Can you still see the white and yolk separately?

Melt some butter or margarine in a small frying pan. Use a *low* flame. Let your child pour the foamy egg into the pan. Teach your child to use a spatula to lift up the edges of the omelet as the egg cooks. Say, "This keeps it from sticking."

If your child wants to scramble the egg, show her how to do it with a fork. Ask her what happens when she scrambles the egg. Ask, "How does an omelet (or scrambled egg) look different from a raw egg?" Help your child learn words like *firmer, fluffier,* and *yellower* to describe changes in the cooking eggs.

Other ways to play the game

When we prepare food, we often *transform* it. The way the food looks, tastes, and feels is changed. Talk with your child about the ways we can transform foods. Heat can change foods. So does freezing. Water changes to ice when we put it in the ice cube tray in the freezer.

Use your kitchen as a science center. Help your child *notice* how foods change when chopped or whipped or blended. Notice how they change when baked, boiled, or fried.

Making mashed potatoes is a good way to show how foods are transformed. Your child can see the steps needed to make hard raw potatoes into fluffy mashed potatoes.

Ask your child to feel uncooked spaghetti before you boil it. Then let her feel the spaghetti after it's cooked. Have her tell you in words how the spaghetti is *changed* by cooking.

Have your child taste, feel, and pull-at a piece of uncooked swiss cheese. Then melt strips of swiss cheese on a piece of bread. Have your child compare the cooked cheese with the uncooked. Ask, "How has the taste and feel changed? What happens when you pull at it?" Your child will enjoy the way cooked swiss cheese pulls like taffy.

Make pancake batter with your children. Using a low flame let the children pour their pancakes on a griddle. Teach them how to notice when a pancake is ready to be turned over. Praise the careful way a child flips a pancake. Why does a pancake need to be turned? How can we tell when a pancake is ready to eat? Does the pancake look like the batter? How do they look different? What changed the batter?

Make applesauce, homemade yogurt, jello, cranberry sauce, bean or lentil soup and other foods. Cooking experience helps children see the changes that happen with heating or chilling foods.

Purpose of the game

Children are puzzled when things are changed or transformed. Young children may not recognize a parent dressed in a strange outfit. They may not recognize a father who grows or who shaves off a beard. They need to learn that people and things can change. Children learn more about how things are the same and how they are different.

Cooking is a fine activity for helping a child learn about how things change. Your child will see how foods are *transformed* by cooking, frying, baking, mashing and freezing.

Your children will learn to reason better if they help with cooking. They can think more clearly about what causes change and what changes they prefer.

- If I like hard boiled eggs, *then* I have to let the egg boil for a *long* time.
- If I cook a hamburger only a short time, *then* the meat stays pink inside. *If* I cook it longer, *then* the meat will look brown and taste well done.

16 Gingerbread Man

What you need

Bits of fruit and raisins
A gingerbread man cookie cutter
A rolling pin
A wooden basting spoon
A greased baking sheet
An oven
A gingerbread mix or recipe

Mix in one bowl:	*Mix in another bowl:*
creamed ⎰ 1 cup soft shortening	5 cups flour
together ⎱ 1 cup brown sugar	2 teaspoons baking soda
1 cup sour milk	1½ teaspoon ginger
¾ cup molasses	1 teaspoon salt
	1 teaspoon cinnamon
	1 tablespoon vinegar

What you do

Read each item of the recipe out loud. Have your *child* measure out all the amounts needed. Show your child how to measure a *level* teaspoon. Show him how to be careful in using spices so they don't spill. Talk about *amounts* such as ½ teaspoon or ¾ cup. *Show* your child how two half-teaspoons of sugar make one teaspoon.

Give your child the basting spoon. Let him blend the shortening and sugar until they are creamy and smooth. Say, "This is called *creaming* the sugar and shortening." Talk about how this creaming *changes* the way the sugar and shortening look. Let the child lick a bit. How does this mixture taste?

Now have your child add the sour milk and molasses. (You can make sour milk by adding a few drops of lemon juice or vinegar to the milk.) Talk about how *slowly* molasses pours. Milk pours faster. Ask your child, "Which looks *thicker*, molasses or milk?"

In another bowl, sift the flour with soda, salt, and spices. Then add the vinegar.

Add the first mixture to the flour and spices mixture. Mix this all together. Keep the dough soft.

Roll out the dough. Let your child use the cookie cutter to cut out gingerbread man shapes. Put each gingerbread man on a greased cookie sheet.

Ask your child, "What does your gingerbread man need to make his face?" Help him find bits of fruit, raisins, nuts, and cinnamon drops. He can use these for eyes, nose, mouth, and coat buttons. Let your child decorate each gingerbread man.

Help your child *count* two eyes, one mouth, three buttons, two legs, two arms, one head.

Chill the dough for several hours. Bake at 350° F for about 15 minutes. Your child may want to taste the dough before and after baking. So set aside a little piece of dough. Can your child describe how the dough tastes different *before* baking and *after* baking?

Other ways to play the game

Baking and cooking are fine times to learn to measure and to count. Include your child often in the counting and measuring that you do in the kitchen. Get him used to measuring *amounts*.

Teach your child cooking words such as —

- a pinch of salt
- paring a potato
- creaming sugar and butter

- cutting an apple into four quarters for four portions.

Have your child count the parts of his body. Talk about the names of the body parts during dressing time or bath time. Count the parts — two hands, ten fingers, one belly button. Ask the child to point to eyes, neck, ears, elbows, and other parts. Can he point to these parts on a doll? Can he easily name body parts on a *picture* of a person? Using a picture may be *harder* for your child than using a real person.

Count as you climb stairs.

Count the number of green peas on your spoon.

Count the number of gingerbread men your recipe makes.

Count the different things in your house. Count slowly *with* your child as you both point to items you are counting. As you begin to count things, also ask your child "What number comes before 3?" or "What number comes after 4?"

Learning to count is hard. Little children do not realize that we must count each item only *once* to get a correct total. Put your finger on each thing and say the number as you count together.

Purpose of the game

Your child will feel very helpful as chef in the kitchen. The good smells and tastes will reward the child's work. He will learn that work is fun and rewarding.

Your child can learn simple ways to measure and count while cooking.

Your child learns many cooking words.

Your child can learn body parts as you make the gingerbread man.

17 Catching a Silly Question: A Learning to Listen Game

What you need

A long list of short questions that take yes or no for an answer

Some questions that are sensible (Use questions like "Do we have eyes?" or "Do fishes swim?")

Some questions that are not sensible, but are mostly silly

What you do

Tell your child you are going to play a question game. The game will show how well she can *listen*. Ask her to answer *yes* or *no* to each question. Tell her, "Some of the questions will make sense. But some will be silly. If you listen carefully you can give the right answer each time. So first listen well. Then answer yes or no."

Here are some ideas for "sillies."

- Do dogs buy groceries?
- Do birds lick ice cream?
- Does water make you thirsty?
- Do shoes go on your hands?
- Do cats bark?
- Do rocks wiggle?
- Do suitcases taste salty?
- Do cows fly?
- Do bunny rabbits sing?
- Do combs brush their teeth?

Be sure to put in some sensible questions that deserve yes answers *between* the "sillies." Then your child will need to listen carefully to catch a "silly."

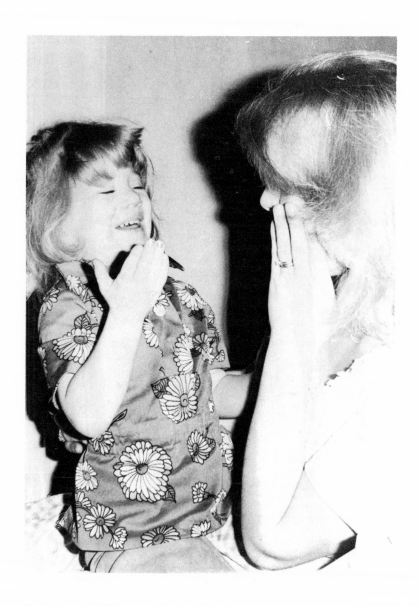

Other ways to play the game

For older children, make up *sensible* questions that sound as if they *might* be "sillies." This will keep your child really listening well. For example:

- Do ballplayers chew?
- Do people ever walk on their hands?

Make up easier "sillies" for younger children.

Purpose of the game

Listening carefully is an important skill in school. This game will help your child listen well, so she can answer well.

18 Frog Friends: A Counting Game

What you need

Four small strips of green celery or green pepper
One bowl of salted water

What you do

Tell your child the story written below about a green frog. Ask your child to *pretend* that the celery or green pepper pieces are green frogs. He can pretend that the bowl of water is a pond.

Help your child learn to add as you tell the story. When you add one frog, count one more number to find out how many frogs you have.

Here's the story:

Once there was a lonesome green frog. Here he is (wiggle your piece of green pepper or celery). He wanted a friend to play with. Can you bring over one friend?

Good! Now how many frogs are here?

Yes, one, two. There are two frogs. There are a *couple* of frogs. After a while the two frogs wanted a friend. Please bring over one more frog — hop, hop, hop.

Thank you. Now there are one, two, *three* frogs.

Now the three frogs decided to do a hop dance. They needed two frogs on one side and two frogs on the other side to dance. See. They need one more frog for their hop dance.

Good. You brought one more frog. Now

there are four. Three frogs plus one more makes four. Two *couples* makes four. Let's make them dance.

Oh, oh. *All* the frogs hear a noise. They are frightened, so they *all* jump into the pond. Can you help the frogs jump into our pond?

Thank you. Now *all* the green frogs are safe in the water. How many are left to play? You are right. Now *none* are left.

If only one frog jumped in the water, then *some* frogs would still be left. (You may want to act out this other ending to the story.)

Other ways to play the game

You can use more pieces of green pepper or celery. This would help an older child learn to count to five or six or more. Just add one piece at a time to the group of frogs.

Ask the child to make one frog at a time *disappear* from the group. The child may eat a piece of celery or pepper to make it go away. Say, "If we take one frog away from four, how many are left?

"Yes, there are three left. And if we eat up one *more*, how many are left?

"Right. Now there are two."

Play this game until there are *no* more frogs. The celery or green pepper is all gone.

Sing the song "One little, two little, three little Indians" with your child. This song carries out the same idea of counting one at a time. It teaches both adding and subtracting.

Purpose of the game

Counting correctly is hard for preschoolers. Playing this game slowly will help teach the idea that we can add on one item to get one number higher. We can take away one item to get one number lower.

Your child will have had a healthy snack when the celery or pepper is eaten.

Your child will learn these words and their meanings: *couple, some, none,* and *all.*

Your child will use imagination to pretend that green pepper strips are frogs.

19 Which Things Do We Do First?

What you need

This game can be played as you talk to your child about daily activities such as —

- dressing for bed
- going to the toilet
- eating meals
- brushing teeth
- washing hair
- other daily routines.

What you do

Help your child become aware of *time* words. Time words include *first, next, last, after,* and *before.* Ask your child questions to find out how well she understands time words. Sometimes ask a silly question. Do this when you are fairly sure that the child knows the correct answer.

Here are some sample questions:

- Do we take off our socks *first,* or our shoes first when we get ready for bed?
- Do we first rinse and rub our hair and *then* shampoo it? Tell me which way we do it.
- Can we take our underpants off *before* we take off our jeans?
- Do we put on hair ribbons *before* we make braids or *after* we make braids?
- When do we rinse out our mouth? Do we do it *after* brushing our teeth or *before* brushing our teeth?

- Do we pull down our pants *after* we go to the toilet or *before* we go?

Use time words as you help your child learn to be patient. She must wait sometimes to get your attention or help. At such times, use words like *soon*, or *in a few minutes*. If you use time words like *later on*, always give a clear idea of what you mean. Otherwise a preschool child finds such words very confusing. You'll make it easier for her if you make clear statements like these:

- I am busy now. *Later* on, *after* I feed the baby, I will come and play ball with you.
- *Right after* I wash out my paint brush and clean up, *then* I will read your story book with you.
- *When* you have finished putting away your toys, then we will be able to go for a walk to the store.

Other ways to play the game

Your child may find these time words easy. Then combine several time words in a sentence. See if the child can understand what you are saying or asking:

- What is the last thing you do when you finish your bath and *before* you put on your pajamas?
- When we make scrambled eggs, what do we do first? Then what do we do right after that?
- You don't like to get shampoo in your eyes. So what must you do *first*, *before* you put the shampoo on your hair?

Help your child think about each step in an activity. Help her see how the steps take place in a certain orderly way. For example, in washing dishes, *first* we scrape plates. *Then* we soap and scrub. Next we rinse. And finally we dry and put away.

Let's say your child has been playing with clay or finger paints. Suppose you two are cleaning the table where she was playing. Both of you have scrubbed the table. The sponge was very soapy. If the table is full of suds, what must you do *next*? Suppose your child wants to color a picture on a sheet of paper now. *Before* the paper is put down, what needs to be done? Yes, *first* we must dry the table. *Then* we can put our sheet of paper down on the clean dry table.

Purpose of the game

Children have a hard time understanding time words that parents use. Words such as *right away, afterward, soon, later,* or *first* puzzle them. But if you use these words daily, it will help. Use them while your child goes about daily activities. Then the child begins to get an idea of how daily time is organized.

Your child will learn what time words mean.

20 Helper around the House

What you need

Jobs around the house that need to be done, such as:

- scouring a pot
- making beds
- washing windows
- cleaning bathtub
- hanging clothes on a line
- drying dishes
- changing vacuum cleaner dirt bag
- sweeping steps
- mopping a kitchen floor
- shampooing a rug

What you do

Tell your child about the job you are both going to be doing today. Explain *what* needs to be done. Tell *why* the family needs this job done. Describe *how* you will do it. Tell your child how he can help. And point out what he must be careful about in doing this job.

In polishing furniture, for example, say, "We must be careful to set the bottle standing up. What happens if the open bottle is lying down? Right! The polish slowly flows out. It could stain a couch or rug badly."

Be sure to admire your child's work as you both get the job done. Exclaim over how shiny the polished table looks. Say how glad you are that he took the smelly garbage out of the kitchen. Act proud that your child found all the correct places to put away each silverware piece. Say, "Now the silverware drawer looks so neat and organized."

Teach your child all the words that belong to each household job. The number of words the child knows will grow. He'll learn words like: *scrub, rake, garbage, furniture polish, sponge mop, tablespoons, rinse,* and *sweep.*

Other ways to play the game

Any household task or yard chore can become a good learning game. Give your child smaller tools to help. Give him a short broom or a small rake, for example.

Make sure you list *all* the steps needed for helping in a task. Perhaps the child is emptying trash cans. Be specific: "First, set down the trash basket near the large garbage barrel. Then lift off the barrel cover. Pour in the trash carefully. Place the cover back on the garbage barrel." Your child will learn that there is often a good, orderly way to do a job.

Purpose of the game

Your child learns that his help counts. He is an important, appreciated member of the family.

Your child learns the different skills needed for different jobs:

- sweeping a floor
- planting seedlings
- sorting clothes
- setting the table
- hanging up tools in a special way

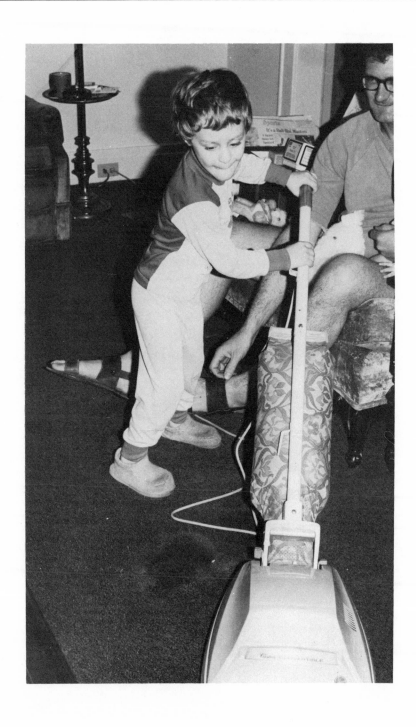

- shoveling snow
- dusting furniture
- folding clothes
- clearing the table

All these jobs help a child become skilled, capable, and graceful.

Each job gives your child a chance to:

- learn new words (Clean windows *sparkle*. Dust collects on *moldings* and *sills*. The baking pans are *stacked* one inside the other. We fold towels and sheets into *rectangles* or *squares*.)
- count items
- learn the order in which a job gets done best
- increase the coordination of eyes and hands and legs and arms.

21 Are There More or Fewer? A Comparing Game

What you need

Pictures cut out from old magazines (Choose objects, people, and animals the child knows well. Pictures of cars, chairs, dogs, boys and girls, and toys will work well.)

Household objects the child knows well

What you do

Help your child learn to compare things.

When your child is putting away toys, ask, "Do you have more cars *or* more toy animals?"

If the child is puzzled, have him line up the toy animals. In front of each animal let the child put a car. Pretend that each animal will need a car for taking a ride. Ask, "Are there any cars left over without animals? Are there any animals left over without cars?"

Suppose there are more cars left over. Say, "These cars are left without animals. That means there are *more* cars than animals. There are *fewer* animals than cars."

Silverware is good for this game. Are there *as many* teaspoons as forks in your trays? Let the child line them up one for one to figure this out. Talk about *comparing* the *number* of spoons with the *number* of forks. There may be a *greater number* of spoons than forks.

Use words to teach your child about the *number* of something compared to something else.

Take out the pictures you have cut out from magazines.

Put out three dogs and four cats. Ask, "Are there *fewer* dogs than cats or *fewer* cats than dogs?" Help your child put a finger on each animal and count. Count the three dogs. Then count the four cats. Explain that *fewer* means there are not as many. Now perhaps the child can answer that there are fewer dogs than cats.

Let the child arrange the pictures. Ask him to arrange the pictures so that there would be fewer cats than dogs. Can the child *think* what must be done? You could *add* more dog pictures. *Or* you could take away some of the cat pictures.

Other ways to play the game

Sit together and look at pictures of picnics or families in a park. Are there more mommies than children? Are there more daddies than sneakers? Help the child to compare total amounts. Count *slowly* together. Have your child put a finger on *each* item counted.

Take a walk and look at the cars parked on your block. Are there more station wagons than other cars? Or are there fewer station wagons? Are there more blue cars than red ones?

This game is easy to play at the store. Are there fewer cooked cereals than ready-to-eat cereals? Are there a *greater number* of frozen orange juice cans than grape juice cans?

Compare furniture and items in your house. Is the number of couches *more than* the number of chairs or *less than* the number of chairs?

When you make a sandwich for lunch, sometimes cut it in half. Compare the number of pieces. There are more small pieces when the sandwich is cut in

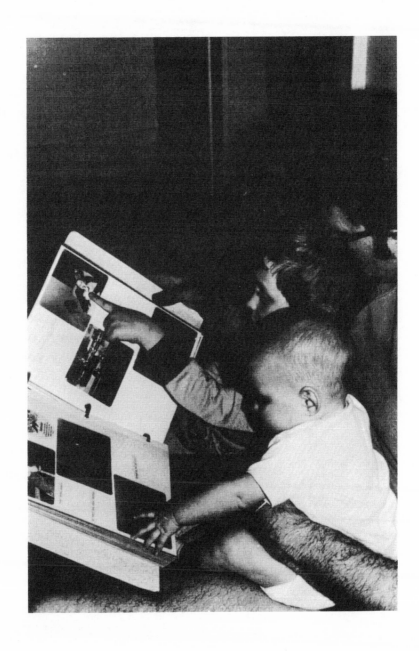

quarters. Count the pieces—one, two, three, four. But there is the same amount of food to eat.

Your child may not understand, so be patient. These ideas are very confusing to a young child.

Use comparison words *only* when you have a clear example to show the child. It's best when the child can handle or clearly see the objects. Then he can try to see for himself how the objects compare.

Purpose of the game

Your child will learn comparison words and meanings.

Your child will learn that amounts may *look* different, but still be the same quantity.

Your child will begin to learn one kind of measuring. He'll learn to line things up in pairs to see if there are the same number.

22 Same and Different: How to Make and Line Up Groups

What you need

A deck of playing cards
Some same- and different-sized empty cans
Some same- and different-sized spoons
Some same- and different-sized carrot sticks
Some same- and different-sized cars and trucks
Some circles that are the same size, but different colors
Some circles that are the same color, but different sizes
Some different-tasting foods, such as lemon and honey
Some foods that taste salty, crunchy, slippery, or sticky
Some buttons of different sizes and kinds
Hardware such as nuts, nails, tacks, screws, and bolts
Plastic sandwich bags or bowls in which to sort objects
A place to take a walk where there are weeds

What you do

Help your child learn when things are the same and when they are different. Help your child learn to group things together. Encourage her to give you a reason why those things go into a group. For example, your child should be able to sort different types of nails and screws into piles. Each pile should have screws or nails that are the same.

Let your child pick up and handle and compare each item. Give her plenty of time to decide whether or not an item belongs in one group or another.

Same-and-different taste games can be played at meal times. Raw carrot sticks are crunchy. What *else* is crunchy? Yes, green peppers, sliced cabbage slaw, and celery! Does spaghetti belong to a group of crunchy foods? Your child should have fun thinking of such an idea.

Some foods taste sweet. Some taste sour and make your mouth feel puckery. Some foods taste smooth, like pudding. Some belong in a group of sticky-tasting foods, like peanut butter or caramels. Some foods taste quite salty. Your child should be able to think of potato chips or pretzels. Some foods are very juicy. Some taste very dry. Some foods can *pour* like milk. Some cannot pour out at all.

Use words that help the child become tuned in to *qualities* that are the *same* or *different*. Be sure to ask your child, "How do you know these are the same? Can you tell me how *these* are different?"

When your child dries dishes, let her sort same and different silverware. Help her put all the teaspoons in one part of the drawer. All the forks go in a different place, and so on.

Sorting toys can be done more naturally during cleanup, just before bedtime. Your child can find all the toy cars and toy trucks. She can pretend a cardboard box is the garage. Let her line up groups of cars and trucks in the garage. All the toy animals can go to sleep in a toy-box or on a shelf. All the dolls can go in another place. Ask your child to tell how she figured out which toys *be-long* together in a group of *same* toys.

You can play this game outdoors by looking for weeds that look the same or different.

Playing cards work well for this game. The child can find *all* the queens or kings in four suits. She can find *all* the red cards with hearts.

Other ways to play the game

Some older children find it easy to sort all the same things according to *one* plan. They will sort things according to:

- the color *or*
- the kind (all cars) *or*
- the use (all tools) *or*
- the shape (all circles) *or*
- the size (all tiny ones) *or*
- whether they go together (cups and saucers).

But even an older child finds it harder to think up *differ-*

ent ways to make groups of things. Suppose your pre-schooler sorts all the little buttons into one pile. She sorts the big buttons into a different pile. Suppose she is even able to *tell* you the idea she used in sorting: "The little

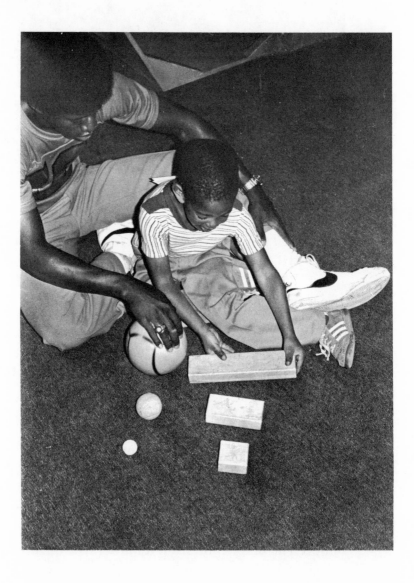

buttons were all the *same.* The big buttons were all the same. So they went into two piles."

Now mix the buttons all together in a pile. Say, "That was good. You figured out that there were big and little buttons. You decided they belonged in different piles. *Now* find *another* way to sort the buttons. Think of a different way to make piles of buttons." See if the child can sort out groups according to *colors* of buttons. Can she make piles of buttons according to the *number of holes* there are to sew the button (two or four holes)? Perhaps your child notices what the buttons are made of. Some are wood, some metal, some plastic. She might sort them according to what they are made of.

Give your child hints and reminders of *differences,* such as color or shape or use or material.

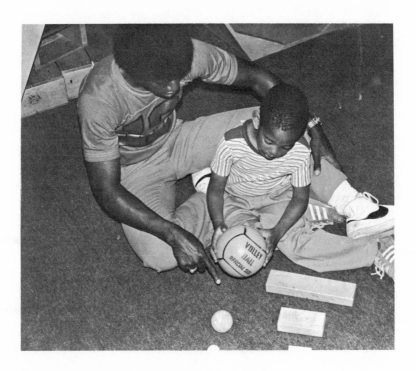

Praise your child for thinking of different ways to make groups.

Another hard idea for the child to understand is that things may be the *same* in one way, but *different* in other ways. Talk about a boat and a car. They are the *same* because they can both take us places. But the boat can go in water and stay on water. The car cannot. It will sink. So they are different.

A girl and a mommy are the same. A boy and a daddy are the same. Yet parents are different from children. They are taller. They have deeper voices. They know lots more about the world. They take care of children.

Lining up games may help your child see how objects in a same group can also be different. Ask your child to take a *same* group, such as red circles or white buttons. Tell her to line them up in order from tiniest to biggest.

This lining up game may be easier with spoons. There are fewer different sizes to line up. The tiny coffee spoon or measuring spoon will be at one end. A big soup ladle may be at the other end of the row. Ask questions to help her: "Where does the teaspoon go? Where does the tablespoon go?" Remind your child to *look* at the spoons all the time to check on the order of lining up. Is it going just right, from smallest to biggest?

This game can be played when sorting clean socks. Some socks are longer than others.

You can snip soda straws into many pieces of different lengths. Teach your child to line up each straw piece at the *edge* of the table. This makes it easier to notice which piece is longer or shorter than another. Help your child look for the shortest straw. Then find the longest straw.

Make this game easier for younger children. It

may be hard for them to line up even three or four lengths of straw exactly from shortest to longest.

Purpose of the game

Your child learns to form groups.

Your child learns to *tell* how she knows that something is the *same* or *different* from another thing.

Your child learns that items can be in the same group and yet be different. Pieces of straw look and feel *alike*, yet they differ in *length*.

Your child learns that sometimes things can go from shortest to tallest. They can go from fattest to skinniest. They can go from littlest to biggest. They can go from lightest to heaviest. They can go from coldest to hottest, and so on. Your child learns to see not just the *big* differences, but the *little differences*. She learns to spot *grades* or *levels* of differences. She learns to put things in order, according to their grades or levels. For example: This straw is shortest. It's first. Then comes this straw. It's a big longer. We'll make it second. Then comes this other straw. It's a bit longer than the second straw. And now we put the longest straw at the other end. It's last.

Your child learns to notice *how* things are the same and how they are different.

Your child learns words that describe different *kinds* of tastes, lengths, shapes, colors, or uses of objects.

23 Neighborhood Explorations

What you need

A walk around the block, or to a park, or for a visit to someone, or in a shopping mall.

What you do

Point out neighborhood numbers and letters to your child wherever you see them. Letters are the building blocks of words. Point out the S in a "STOP" sign, the G in a "GAS" sign, the B in "BUS STOP," the letters on automobile license plates, the E in "EXIT," the N in "NO PARKING," the W in "ONE WAY" signs. These street signs make it easy to use your neighborhood to begin teaching the letters of our alphabet. Find sign letters that are the same as letters in your child's name.

Count with your child all the sidewalk lines stepped on, or stepped over. Count the numbers of houses on the street.

Talk about houses. Talk about sloping or flat roofs. Ask your child if she notices the triangle shape of an attic room. Discuss shingles and bricks and stucco and siding.

Talk about the different kinds of ways to travel. You are walking. But there are other ways to travel. In a car, a truck, a bus. Can your child spot different kinds of riding vehicles on the road? Ask your child to think up other ways to go. Children can hop or skip, ride a tricycle or pull each other in a wagon. Some little children you meet on the street may be riding in a stroller or a carriage.

Play a game of "Guess who lives in that house" as

you pass a house. Sharpen your child's noticing skills. If there is a small tricycle parked in the driveway or a ten-speed bike with books in a basket, who is likely to live there? Being able to make good guesses and give reasons for them are important thinking skills.

If an airplane rumbles overhead or people are dumping trash from barrels into garbage trucks ask your child to *describe* what is happening?

Feel the bark of trees. Talk about smooth and rough feeling bark. If your child closes eyes and you brush her hand along a bush can your child describe *what* was felt?

If you are shopping, model words that are polite. "Could you please show me this sandal in a size 7?" "Could you please put our groceries in a double bag since we have a long way to walk and we want to be sure the groceries don't break through the bag."

Other ways to play the game

Plan family trips to the zoo or library or park. Talk about what you will need to get ready to to bring with you. Plan a picnic outdoors. Ask your child to *plan* with you. What will you need to bring? How can you keep juice from spilling? How can you keep milk cold? How many paper plates will you need? A picnic can be held in a backyard or on a porch or at a friend's house.

If you take a bus, train or car trip outside your neighborhood then you can see even more scenery and actions and people to talk about with your child. Answer your child's questions the best you can. For pre-schoolers, taking a ride is an adventure. There are so many new things to see and to be curious about. Nourish your child's sense of wonder about the world. Just seeing a cow in a field can cause a two-year-old to become joyful and talkative. Just seeing the way a bus driver maneuvers in traffic can make a six-year-old curious to know how different cars and buses are to operate.

Take advantage of special free events in your community such as an outdoor crafts show, a rose garden display, a parade, a children's museum display or a puppet show in the local library. Remember that small children tire easily and need to eat at meal times. Plan your outing so that your child can enjoy the new experience. Talk about whatever strikes the imagination or excites interest. Sometimes a small child will enjoy very different aspects of a trip compared to adults. The adult may be awed by scenic wonders. The child may be pleased with new rocks she has picked for her collection.

Purpose of the game

Neighborhood visits and explorations enlarge experience. Your child can learn new words like "telephone pole" or "poison ivy" or "curb" or "oil delivery truck" that cannot be easily learned indoors except with pictures. Neighborhood language games build your child's vocabulary and store of experiences. Then in school, when your child comes across some of these words in readers these words will already represent familiar items and happenings.

Neighborhood explorations will give your child adventures to share with family and friends. During meal time conversations your child will have experiences to recall and to relate.

Using slides or see-saws in the park will give your child opportunities for friendly play, for taking turns, and for sharing an activity together with playmates.

24 Social Skills

What you need

Learning to get along peacefully and happily with other people is very important. To help your child learn this, first, you need to make time for loving and for giving *personal* attention to your child.

From the time a child is a tiny baby, he is learning how *you* feel about being a parent. Your happy feelings toward your child are very important. *Your* good feelings will help your children grow up with good feelings about themselves and about other people.

Second, you need to set a good example. *Be* the kind of person you would like your child to become. Do you want a patient, helpful, kind child? Then be patient, helpful, and kind. Be a good winner and a good loser. Your child loves you and will copy you.

If you are a caring, sharing person, your child will want to be that way, too. If you say *please* and *thank you*, your child is more likely to use those words, too.

Third, you need a set of *rules* for solving personal troubles. A parent who uses reasonable ways to solve personal problems will be able to help a child gain problem-solving skills. Fighting, yelling, and scolding may only lead to worse problems later.

What you do

Show your children in small everyday actions that you are *glad* to be their daddy or mommy.

Help your child to feel wanted and cared for in your family.

Act with other people in ways that are good for a child to copy. Be a helpful neighbor. Act kind and patient with people who are slower or clumsier than you. Your child will notice your ways. Make little gifts and cards for friends and family for special holidays or celebrations. Prepare for visits to other families. Before you go, talk about how to act with other people and with their things.

Treat people as if you care what happens to them. Ask for things in a friendly way, so that others will *want* to do things for you. Your child picks up *your* manner of talking and asking for things.

Use positive rules to solve your own problems. If you have a problem, try to figure out *what* the problem is. Find out *how* you are feeling. Are you angry, scared, jealous, or cranky? Then try to figure out how you can *change* your trouble. How can you get your needs met in reasonable ways? Screaming, giving the cold-silent treatment, hitting, and escaping are not reasonable ways.

When you are in conflict with someone, try to figure out how the other person is feeling too. Try to decide how *you* will act and feel, depending on what the other person does and says. Then figure out what may happen *after that*. Looking ahead like this, may help you find more reasonable ways to solve a problem with another person.

Now try these ideas with your child when he faces trouble with others. Teach your child how to figure out *what* the problem is. What is your child feeling? Help him talk about his feelings. How is the other child feeling? Let your child tell you.

Help your child figure out what will happen if they try to settle their mad feelings by hitting a playmate.

Many children do not think clearly about emotional troubles. A boy may have your child's toy car. Your child may hit the boy and grab the car back. Once a fight begins, maybe the other child will be sent home. Then there is no more play time together that day. Help your child *think* before using hitting. What is another way your child can think of to solve this conflict? How can he get back his toy *without* a fight?

If your child has a good answer to these questions, urge him to try it out. Your child might say, "I know. He can have my truck to play with. Then he will give me back my car."

If one idea doesn't work out, have your child try to think of another idea. It is important to *help your child think up different ways to solve problems*. If a child *thinks* before acting in hurting ways, then she has a chance to find a better way. She can think of a good way to solve the problem that's making her feel angry.

When your child has strong feelings, help him *put those feelings into words*. Help him describe his an-

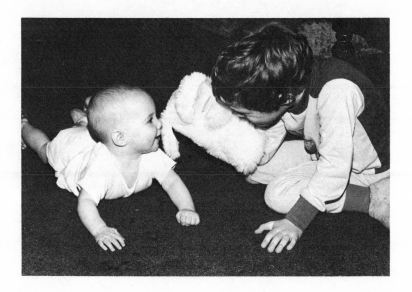

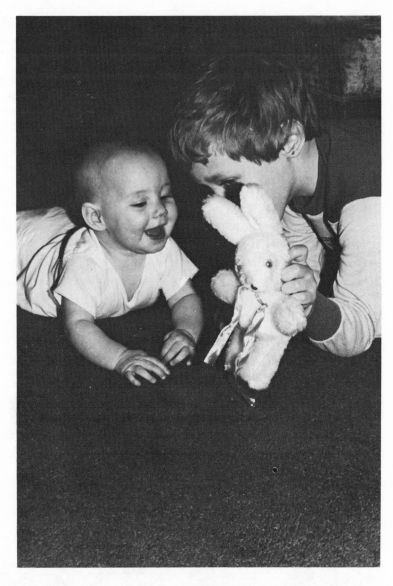

ger, happiness, or sadness. Ask your child to tell you what happened. Find out the reasons for the bad feelings. Help your child *talk* about the problem he is having. Don't preach or criticize. Just try to tune in to your child's feelings and concerns. Often a child can solve his own problem if he just has an understanding parent who will listen carefully to those troubled feelings.

Purpose of the game

Children who are happy in their feelings and in their social life can get along easier in life. They have *energy to learn* and study. Their energy is not used up in being angry or scared.

Your children will learn to express their glad feelings and their bad feelings. You may quite rightly forbid your child to act in hurtful ways. But your child will learn that he has a right to have whatever *feelings* are there.

Children need social skills. Politeness helps us get where we want to in life. Your child will learn socially polite ways to ask for things. He will learn words to greet and thank other people. He will learn ways to compliment people.

Teachers and other children will enjoy your child's company more. A teacher will be very glad to have your child in class. The teacher will greatly appreciate your child's positive social skills.

Your child will learn how to *think* of many different ways to solve personal troubles with others. Your child will become a creative problem solver.

If you play this game well, then someday your child will be playing it with your grandchild. Your child will grow up to become a loving, teaching parent who will help your grandchild become a good learner and a good person.

PLAYTIME LEARNING GAMES FOR YOUNG CHILDREN

was composed in 12-point Compugraphic Caledonia and leaded two points,
with display type in Caledonia and Helvetica,
by Metricomp Studios;
printed on 55-pound, acid-free Glatfelter Antique Cream paper stock,
adhesive-bound with 10-point Carolina covers, printed and laminated by Philips Offset,
by Maple-Vail Book Manufacturing Group, Inc.;
and published by

SYRACUSE UNIVERSITY PRESS
SYRACUSE, NEW YORK